GAME TIME: NOTES OF ENCOURAGEMENT TO MY GRANDSON

by Olivia Wilkinson

TRILOGY

Game Time: Notes of Encouragement to My Grandson

Trilogy Christian Publishers A Wholly Owned Subsidary of Trinity Broadcasting Network

2442 Michelle Drive Tustin, CA 92780

Rights Department, 2442 Michelle Drive, Tustin, CA 92780.

Trilogy Christian Publishing/TBN and colophon are trademarks of Trinity Broadcasting Network.

Cover design by: Natalee Dunning

For information about special discounts for bulk purchases, please contact Trilogy Christian Publishing.

Trilogy Disclaimer: The views and content expressed in this book are those of the author and may not necessarily reflect the views and doctrine of Trilogy Christian Publishing or the Trinity Broadcasting Network.

Manufactured in the United States of America

10 9 8 7 6 5 4 3 2 1

Library of Congress Cataloging-in-Publication Data is available.

ISBN: 978-1-68556-131-4

E-ISBN: 978-1-68556-132-1

TABLE OF CONTENTS

Bring Your Best Game Every Time!

September 18, 2015

No matter how the game is going, continue to bring your best game. If you continue to do this, you will win every time. Your prize is not in your last game; your prize is always before you. When you go into the locker room at halftime, come out saying, "Come on, Jesus!"

When you win, do not be prideful or boastful. Be quietly and prayerfully thankful to God. You are a gift from God. Your talent is a gift from God. Your strength and power are gifts from God.

We are so proud of you and pleased with your accomplishments. You have such a loving, kind, and gentle spirit in that strong and powerful body. We love you so much; we hardly have any left for anyone else.

Praying for God's blessings on you always,

Love,

Odah and Grandad

⁓

First Corinthians 9:24 (NASB) says, "Do you not know that those who run in a race all run, but *only* one receives the prize? Run in such a way that you may win!"

Audience of One

October 2, 2015

Do not be swayed by the noise of the stadium crowds, for they will leave and forget all about you and the game.

Do remember there is always an audience of one. God is an audience of one. He is always watching to see that you do your best with what He has given you. You are an audience of one. You are always watching to make sure that you do your best.

The scout is an audience of one. The scout is always watching to see what kind of game you are bringing. Don't compare yourself with anyone else. Just be the best Elijah you can be!

You will win every time when you play for your audience of one.

Praying for God's blessings on your life always,

Love,

Granddad and Odah

❧

Joshua 1:9 (NIV) says, "Have I not commanded you? Be strong and courageous. Do not be terrified; do not be discouraged, for the Lord your God will be with you wherever you go."

Gratitude

October 10, 2015

"Gratitude is a spiritual magnet. I put my attention on the positive and draw more of the same to me." Friends, family, teammates, coaches, and the comfort of home bless you every day. Live from a place of gratitude and find an abundance of joy! At times you may feel less than blessed. You may face financial or health challenges. If you are going through a transition and feel lost or confused because of the disappointing results of a football game, refocus on gratitude. Make a list of five things for which you are grateful. As you think about your blessings, your attitude changes. You attract more blessings as you practice gratitude.

God bless you, your team, and your coaches. We are grateful to all of you!

Love and blessings always,

Granddad and Odah

First Thessalonians 5:16–18 (NIV) says, "Be joyful always, pray continually, give thanks in all circumstances, for this is God's will for you in Christ Jesus."

WINNING ON THE INSIDE
October 23, 2015

Keep your confidence up because God made you competent to succeed in this, your chosen career. There is a story about a little boy whose mom told him to sit down. He told his mom, "I may be sitting down on the outside, but I am standing up on the inside!" On the outside, the team is losing, but on the inside, you are still a winner because you brought your best game and your offensive team put points on the board! We will be watching for the great sixty-eight and, yes, praying for a win for the Minutemen! God bless your team and the coaches with the strength, endurance, and wisdom to win this game!

Love,
Granddad and Odah

God Is Calling the Shots
October 31, 2015

You are God's dream wrapped up in Elijah! Failures, defeats, and trials are all tests to make you stronger (mentally, physically, and spiritually). It takes a lifetime to work out God's dream, so do not grow tired or impatient with doing your best.

"So let us not become tired of doing good; for if we do not give up, the time will come when we will reap the harvest" (Galatians 6:9, GNT).

God is calling the shots. He knows you can pass them. He wants *you* to know what you can do. We will be watching and praying for a win today!

God bless your coaches and team with the strength, endurance, and wisdom needed to win.

Love and blessings always,
Granddad and Odah

Psalm 27:14 (KJV) says, "Wait on the Lord: Be of good courage, and He shall strengthen thine heart. Wait, I say, on the Lord."

Lil' Ragin' Bull

November 2, 2015

Your first football coach, Colin, prophesied you by nicknaming you, "Lil' Ragin' Bull!" Your demeanor in your first football picture confirms that you already agreed with him.

It is not just about reaching your goals. It is also about who you become while achieving those goals. On the way, you are building a reputation of integrity, perseverance, leadership, and more! You are also learning how to lose graciously.

Don't worry about the haters. If you have no haters, you are not that gifted. If you have a gift, there is a place created for it. Your gift will make room for you. Don't let the slackers or games lost get you down. You keep showing up and showing out!

Proverbs 18:16 (NASB) says, "A man's gift makes room for him, and brings him before great men."

The Audition Continues!

November 9, 2015

When difficult times come into your life, what is your response?

While it may look tempting to look for a shortcut out of the discomfort, that's not the kind of attitude God desires from us. Instead, He wants his children to remain submitted to Him, though that may not end the affliction. But it is the Lord's will that we hold our heads high and press on through the pain.[1]

"Blessed (happy, to be envied) is the man who is patient under trial and stands up under temptation, for when he has stood the test and been approved, he will receive the victor's crown of life which God has promised to those who love him" (James 1:12, AMPC).

You will get through this! It won't be painless. It won't be quick. We share your pain now and will support you all the way. God bless your coaches and team with the strength, endurance, and wisdom needed to win.

Love and blessings always,
Granddad and Odah

---

1. In Touch Magazine, Daily Reading, 11/9/15

YOU ARE RIGHT ON TRACK
AND YOU ARE RIGHT IN STEP!

November 20, 2015

"The steps of good men are directed by the Lord. He delights in each step they take. If they fall, it isn't fatal, for the Lord holds them with His hand" (Psalm 37:23–25, TLB).

Love and blessings always,

Granddad and Odah

From Dream to Destiny

September 17, 2016

We are praying for you to make good decisions, use wisdom, and stay on God's path for your life. God gave you this dream since you were a toddler, don't let the world take it away from you. Don't try to satisfy yourself with things that never satisfy anybody. You are too close to losing it all now!

God gave you your gift to do what you do. When you were at DW, they thought you possessed more talent than any other player. Your gift will make room for you if you have patience and self-control.

"And let us not lose heart and grow weary and faint in acting nobly and doing right, for in due time and at the appointed season we shall reap, if we do not loosen and relax our courage and faint" (Galatians 6:9, AMPC).

Remember that every decision you make has consequences. Consequences tell a story about you, and some of them can wreck your life! Make better decisions, and you will have fewer regrets. Every time you make a decision, ask yourself these questions: Does this honor God, me, my coach, my team, or my family? Finally, does this decision help me realize my dream and my destiny?

Be honest with yourself and make the right decision. Your future is in your hands!

Love and blessings always,

Granddad and Odah (your grandmom)

Keep the Faith

October 13, 2016

Keep faith in God that your destiny is being fulfilled. Don't waste time regretting mistakes. Count the lessons learned from them as rungs in your ladder leading to your destiny. No matter how the rung was made of joy or sorrow, of failure or success, of wounds or healing, as long as it served its purpose to advance you to your goal.

Learn from your mistakes, and keep your faith in God that you are on the right path to fulfill your destiny

Psalm 34:4–7 (NLT) says, "I prayed to the Lord, and He answered me. He freed me from all my fears. Those who look to Him for help will be radiant with joy; no shadow of shame will darken their faces. In my desperation, I prayed, and the Lord listened; He saved me from all my troubles. For the angel of the LORD is a guard; he surrounds and defends all who fear him."

March 19, 2017

Dear friends,

Please pray for my grandson, Elijah. He has had a strong desire to play football since he was a toddler. He used to put on his older brother's football uniform and tackle him across the floor. Now he has played from toddler all the way through college. On Thursday, March 23, 2017, his university is having its Pro Day. Please pray with me that Elijah will have a very successful day! Thank you for your prayers.

Love and blessings,
Olivia Wilkinson

May 19, 2017

Thank God for answered prayer! Elijah has finished college and received a three-year contract with an NFL team! We can't stop praising the Lord! Thank you for your prayers!

Love and blessings,

Olivia Wilkinson

I Go Out and I Come In

August 1, 2017

"I go out and I come in." (This is a phrase used in the Old Testament which refers to war.)

As you go out to practice for a game (battle), meditate on Joshua 1:9, translated into the first person: "I am strong and courageous. I am not terrified; I am not discouraged, for the Lord my God is with me wherever I go."

When you come in from practice or a game (battle), meditate on Psalm 44:4–8 (NIV) translated into the first person: "You are my King and my God, who decrees victories for Elijah. Through you, I push back my enemies; through your name I trample my foes. You give me victory over my enemies, you put my adversaries to shame. In God I make my boast all day long, and I will praise Your name forever."

Joshua 1:9 gives you strength, courage, and faith before the battle.

Psalm 44:4–8 gives God praise, thanks, and worship for keeping you, strengthening you, and building your faith through the battle.

Faith

August 7, 2017

Thoughts from Andrew Womack's program on Monday, August 7, 2017:

Faith is seeing into the future. Faith is the ability to see what is happening right now in the unseen realm.

What is God speaking to you? The things that God has shown you are eternal. What God has shown you will come to pass!

Your job is to keep showing up and doing your best!

Do the Next Best Thing!

September 2, 2017

Relax and do the next best thing! God also leads by shutting doors! Let us thank God that you have had four months to be in the spotlight with the Denver Broncos. When one door closes, a better one opens! Revelations 3:7–8 (NIV) says, "What he opens no one can shut, and what he shuts no one can open. I know your deeds. See, I have placed before you an open door that no one can shut." He has opened the door to the NFL!

Live Your Dream!

October 22, 2017

Let us give thanks to God for allowing you to live your dream with the Denver Broncos. Just go on that field and be the best Elijah you can be!

Joshua 1:9 (NIV) says, "Have I not commanded you? Be strong and courageous. Do not be terrified; do not be discouraged, for the Lord your God will be with you wherever you go."

Revelations 3:7–8 (NIV) says, "These are the words of Him who is holy and true, who holds the key of David. What He opens no one can shut, and what He shuts no one can open. I know your deeds. See, I have placed before you an open door that no one can shut."

God has opened the door to the NFL for you! Now, walk through it with Him!

GAME TIME!

October 30, 2017

Bring your best game every time!

No matter how the team is doing or how the game is going, continue to bring your best game.

Your prize is not in your last game; your prize is always before you. It's never too late to win!

Psalm 144:1–2 (NIV) says, "Praise be to the Lord my Rock, who trains my hands for war, my fingers for battle. He is my loving God and my fortress, my stronghold and my deliverer, my shield, in whom I take refuge, who subdues people under me."

Win or Lose!

November 4, 2017

As always, be the best Elijah you can be. Be grateful! Be humble! You are truly living your dream! You are in *Philadelphia*, your hometown, *playing the Eagles*!

Win or lose, you are a winner!

Isaiah 40:29–31 (GNT) says, "He strengthens those who are weak and tired. Even those who are young grow weak; young people can fall exhausted. But those who trust in the Lord for help will find their strength renewed. They will rise on wings like eagles; they will run and not get weary; they will walk and not grow weak."

Be blessed and give thanks to God!

DIVINE ORDER

November 5, 2017

Relax! You are in Divine order! You are in God's order! The man who fears God has nothing else to fear. He has a plan for you, to give you a future and hope. Go with God. He goes with you!

Psalm 91:11–13 (NIV) says, "For He will command His angels concerning you to guard you in all your ways; they will lift you up in their hands, so that you will not strike your foot on a stone. You will tread upon the lion and the cobra; you will trample the great lion and the serpent."

Never forget:

Joshua 1:9 says, "Have I not commanded you? Be strong and courageous. Do not be terrified; do not be discouraged, for the Lord your God will be with you wherever you go."

Be Ready!

November 9, 2017

Be ready in season and out of season!

Be ready physically, mentally, and *spiritually*.

"…This is the Word of the Lord to Zerubbabel: 'Not by might, nor by power, but by my Spirit,' says the Lord Almighty" (Zechariah 4:6, NIV).

Excellent Prayer!

November 11, 2017

Lord, with all my heart I thank you. I will sing your praises before the armies of angels. I face your Temple as I worship, giving thanks to you for all your loving-kindness and your faithfulness, for your promises are backed by all the honor of your name. When I pray, you answer me, and encourage me by giving me the strength I need. Every king in all the earth shall give you thanks, O Lord, for all of them shall hear your voice. Yes, they shall sing about Jehovah's glorious ways, for His glory is very great. Yet though He is so great, He respects the humble, but proud men must keep their distance. Though I am surrounded by troubles, you will bring me safely through them. You will clench your fist against my angry enemies! Your power will save me. The Lord will work out His plans for my life—for your loving-kindness, Lord, continues forever. Don't abandon me—for you made me.

Psalm 138 (TLB)

STRENGTH!

November 12, 2017

Thank you, God, for your Word. Your Word gives me strength... strength in my mind, body, and spirit.

Joshua 1:9 (NIV) says, "Have I not commanded you? Be strong and courageous. Do not be terrified; do not be discouraged, for the Lord your God will be with you wherever you go."

Protected!

November 19, 2017

Psalm 91:14–15 says, "Because He loves me, says the Lord, I will rescue him; I will protect him, for he acknowledges my name. He will call upon me and I will answer him; I will be with him in trouble, I will deliver him and honor him."

Keeping my focus on God protects me. I am the director of my thoughts. At times my attention may dwell on old messages I hear in my head. Yet, the Spirit reminds me that I have the ability to focus my attention on the divine truth available to me through my oneness with God.

I focus on divine love within me, and any illusion I have of being alone or afraid is eradicated! Focused on God, I am at peace!

In Due Time

December 2, 2017

You are in the *right* place, at the *right* time, with the *right* people! God led you here.

Continue to make good decisions, use wisdom, and stay on His path; then, He will lead you higher. There were many things for you to learn on this difficult path. Learn them well. Then, He will make your path straight and continue to lead you *right*!

Galatians 6:9 (the Book and NIV) says, "And let us not get tired of doing what is right, for *in due time* we will reap a harvest of blessings if we do not get discouraged and give up."

Forget the Past and Reach to the Goal!

December 3, 2017

Bring your best game every time!

No matter how the game is going or how the team is doing, continue to bring your best game. Your prize is not in your last game; your prize is always before you.

It's never too late to win!

Philippians 3:13–14 (the Book and NASB) says, "No, dear brothers, I am still not all I should be, but I am bringing all my energies to bear on this one thing: Forgetting the past and looking forward to what lies ahead, I press on towards the goal for the prize of the upward call of God in Christ Jesus."

Never forget:

Joshua 1:9 says, "Have I not commanded you? Be strong and courageous. Do not be terrified; do not be discouraged, for the Lord your God will be with you wherever you go."

Thankful! Grateful!

December 10, 2017

Psalm 100:4–5 (TLB) says, "Go through his gates with great thanksgiving; enter His courts with praise. Give thanks to Him and bless His name. For the Lord is always good. He is always loving and kind, and His faithfulness goes on and on to each succeeding generation."

My life is filled with an overflowing measure of God's blessings. I am grateful, and I give thanks to God. His divine healing energy flows through my body, and I embrace the peace that washes over me when challenges appear. The practice of gratitude draws ever more abundance to me. My spirit is at peace and is fulfilled.[2]

Always remember Joshua 1:9 (TLB), "Yes, be bold and strong! Banish fear and doubt! For remember, the Lord your God is with you wherever you go."

---

2. Excerpts from DW, 12-9-17.

Nobody but God!

2018

God has given you a favor! When God favors you, He works in your life in ways you cannot explain. God has opened this door.

Revelation 3:7–8 (NIV) says, "To the angel of the church in Philadelphia write: These are the words of the One who is holy and true, who holds the key of David. What He opens no one can shut, and what He shuts no one can open. I know what you do; I know that you have a little power; you have followed my teaching and have been faithful to me. I have opened a door in front of you, which no one can close."

Now walk through it with God's blessings and strength, and power.

Be blessed and give God honor.

The Holy Spirit Is with You!

August 11, 2018

The Holy Spirit is with you, and He is directing your paths! Don't let the unholy spirit throw you off your game! He will show up disguised as a jealous teammate, a bully, a racist, etc. When you recognize him, remember this prayer for your life: "We pray that you will make good decisions, use wisdom and stay on God's path for your life."

Proverbs 3:5–6 (NKJV) says, "Trust in the Lord with all your heart, And lean not on your own understanding; In all your ways acknowledge Him, And He shall direct your paths."

Proverbs 4:5, 7–9 (NKJV) says, "Get wisdom! Get understanding! Wisdom is the principal thing…Therefore get wisdom. And in all your getting, get understanding. Exalt her (wisdom) and she will promote you; She will bring you honor, when you embrace her. She will place on your head an ornament of Grace; a crown of Glory she will deliver to you."

FIRST DAY!

September 1, 2018

Today is the first day of the rest of your life! Play like it's overtime! "Take delight in the Lord, and He will give you your heart's desires. Commit everything you do to the Lord. Trust Him, and He will help you" (Psalm 37:4–5).

"This is my command: Be strong and courageous! Do not be afraid or discouraged. For the Lord your God is with you wherever you go" (Joshua 1:9).

Go with God! He goes with you. When approaching a difficult situation, say to yourself, "Come on, Jesus!" He is in there (you)!

WAIT!

September 23, 2018

Do not become impatient. God will give you a time and a place to shine. Good things come to those who wait!

Psalm 27:14 (KJV) says, "Wait on the Lord: be of good courage, and He shall strengthen your heart: wait, I say, on the Lord."

Psalm 130:5 (NIV) says, "I wait for the Lord, my soul waits, and in His Word I put my hope."

Isaiah 40:29–31 (NASB) says, "He gives strength to the weary, / And to him who lacks might He increases power. / Though youths grow weary and tired, / And vigorous young men stumble badly, / Yet those who wait for the Lord / Will gain new strength; / They will mount up with wings like eagles, / They will run and not get tired, / They will walk and not become weary."

Never forget!

Joshua 1:9 (NIV) says, "Have I not commanded you? Be strong and courageous. Do not be terrified; do not be discouraged, for the Lord your God will be with you wherever you go."

STANDBY!

October 1, 2018

Standby: Readiness for duty or immediate deployment, ready to act immediately when called upon. You are on standby for the Broncos just as the Holy Spirit is on standby for you. The Holy Spirit is ready to jump in to help you whenever He is called. You are ready to jump in to help the Broncos whenever you are called.

John 14:16 (AV) says, "And I will ask the Father, and He will give you another comforter (counselor, helper, intercessor, advocate, strengthener, and *standby*) that He may remain with you forever. The Spirit of Truth…"

Another Standby: Joshua 1:9 says, "Have I not commanded you? Be strong and courageous. Do not be terrified, do not be discouraged, for the Lord your God will be with you wherever you go."

READY

October 6, 2018

Ready: In a suitable state for an activity, action, or situation; fully prepared.

Synonym: Set, fit, psyched up, geared up.

You must stay ready because the call will come when you least expect it. But you can relax! You are in divine order, which is God's order! The man who fears God has nothing else to fear. He has a plan for you, to give you a future and hope. Go with God. He goes with you!

Psalm 91:11–13 (NIV) says, "For He will concern His angels concerning you to guard you in all your ways; they will lift you up in their hands, so that you will not strike your foot on a stone. You will tread upon the lion and the cobra; you will trample the great lion and the serpent."

Never forget:

"Have I not commanded you? Be strong and courageous. Do not be terrified; do not be discouraged, for the Lord your God will be with you wherever you go" (Joshua 1:9, NIV).

Your Best Game!

October 13, 2018

Your best game is ahead of you. Equip yourself to rise to the top of your profession: Practice! Practice! Practice!

There are forces set up to tempt you to make choices that will prevent you from reaching the top. Do not dwell on the past. Use the past to learn from mistakes, then move forward!

Always stay humble. "Humble yourself in the sight of the Lord, and He shall lift you up" (James 5:10, KJV).

Always stay thankful with a grateful heart.

"Enter His gates with thanksgiving and His courts with praise; give thanks to Him and praise His name. For the Lord is good and His love endures forever; His faithfulness continues through all generations" (Psalm 100:4–5, NIV).

Before every battle, take the Word of God! "Have I not commanded you? Be strong and courageous. Do not be terrified; do not be discouraged, for the Lord your God will be with you wherever you go" (Joshua 1:9, NIV).

RECALL!

October 18, 2018

Recall: To bring back awareness or attention as to the immediate situation.

Recall past victories.

Recall who brought you this far.

"You are my king and my God who decrees victories for Elijah. Through you I push back my enemies; through your name I trample my foes. You give me victory over my enemies, you put my adversaries to shame. In God I make my boast all day long, and I will praise your name forever" (Psalm 44:4–8, NIV, translated into the first person).

He didn't bring you this far to only bring you this far, and you didn't come this far to only come this far!

Battle cry: "Have I not commanded you? Be strong and courageous. Do not be terrified; do not be discouraged, for the Lord your God will be with you wherever you go" (Joshua 1:9, NIV).

DIVINE ORDER!

November 3, 2018

Relax! You are in Divine Order! You are in God's Order! The man who fears God has nothing else to fear. He has a plan for you, to give you a future and hope. Go with God. He goes with you!

Psalm 91:11–13 (NIV) says, "For He will command His angels concerning you to guard you in all your ways; they will lift you up in their hands, so that you will not strike your foot on a stone. You will tread upon the lion and the cobra; you will trample the great lion and the serpent."

Never forget:

Battle cry: "Have I not commanded you? Be strong and courageous. Do not be terrified; do not be discouraged, for the Lord your God is with you wherever you go" (Joshua 1:9, NIV).

Another Milestone!

November 17, 2018

Another milestone was reached! And the audition continues! You are playing for the Denver Broncos in two positions! Your gifts are surely making room for you. Your Heavenly Father put this dream in your heart. Now, it is up to you to live it out. Keep walking towards God, and you will fulfill your destiny.

I Go Out and I Come In (2)

December 2, 2018

"I go out and I come in" (This is a phrase used in the Old Testament which refers to war.)

As you go out to practice or a game (battle), meditate on Joshua 1:9, translated into the first person, "I am bold and strong! I banish fear and doubt! I remember the Lord my God is with me wherever I go."

When you come in from practice or a game (battle), meditate on Psalm 44:4–8 (NIV) translated into the first person, "You are my king and my God, who decrees victories for Elijah. Through you I push back my enemies; through your name I trample my foes. You give me victory over my enemies, you put my adversaries to shame. In God I make my boast all day long, and I will praise your name forever."

Joshua 1:9 gives you strength, courage, and faith before the battle.

Psalm 44:4–8 gives God praise, thanks, and worship for keeping you, strengthening you, and building your faith throughout the battle.

Ready, Set, Go

December 15, 2018

You won three in a row, now let's go win three more! You know how, just do what you did before! Play like it's overtime! "Take delight in the Lord, and He will give you your heart's desires. Commit everything you do to the Lord. Trust Him, and He will help you" (Psalm 37:4–5).

He didn't bring you this far to only bring you this far, and you didn't come this far to only come this far!

Always remember Joshua 1:9 (NIV), "Have I not commanded you? Be strong and courageous. Do not be terrified; do not be discouraged, for the Lord your God will be with you wherever you go."

Battle cry: "I am bold and strong! I banish fear and doubt! I remember the Lord my God is with me wherever I go!" (Joshua 1:9, TLB).

Go Broncos! Keep on winning! Come on, Jesus!

KEEP ON DREAMING!

December 24, 2018

Dream: A strongly desired goal or purpose

To dream: To imagine as possible!

Proverbs 29:18 (Amplified) says, "Where there is no vision (dream) the people perish; but he who keeps the law (rules), blessed, happy and fortunate is he."

Proverbs 13:12 says, "Hope deferred makes the heart sick, but a dream fulfilled is a tree of life."

Proverbs 13:19–20 says, "It is pleasant to see dreams come true, but fools refuse to turn from evil to attain them. Walk with the wise and become wise; associate with fools and get in trouble."

Do not let anyone or anything steal your dream, and do not destroy it yourself! Only *you* can fulfill *your dream*. No matter where *you* are today, remember what Romans 8:28 (NASB) says, "And we know that God causes all things to work together for good for those who love God, to those who are called according to His purpose."

Today, *your dream* continues at Oakland-Alameda County Coliseum! Be the best Elijah you can be in *your dream*! Always remember Joshua 1:9 (NIV), "Have I not commanded you?

Be strong and courageous. Do not be discouraged; do not be terrified, for the Lord your God is with you wherever you go."

Battle cry: "I am bold and strong! I banish fear and doubt! I remember the Lord my God is with me wherever I go!" (Joshua 1:9, TLB).

Go, Broncos! Win, Broncos! Stay in the hunt! Come on, Jesus!

THE JOY OF THE LORD IS YOUR STRENGTH
August 9, 2019

Dear Grandson,

The last two pictures, one from the Denver Post and one from the Broncos' website, have prompted me to write to you. They suggest to me that you are downcast in spirit. Always remember who is living inside of your spirit. The Holy Spirit lives inside of you, and He brings the fruit of the Spirit: love, joy, peace, patience, kindness, goodness, faithfulness, gentleness, and self-control into your life. Use your faith to be patient. You are on a journey with Him. No one can take your good from you. What God has planned for you will come if you wait on Him. With every wait, there is a suddenly! Recall some of your *suddenlies*! As an old lady once told me, "I dare you to trust Him!" Now your old grandmom is telling you, "I dare you to trust Him!"

Love and blessings always,

Odah

In Scriptures, Psalm 37:4–7[3] says, "Delight yourself in the Lord and He will give you the desires of your heart. Commit your way to the Lord; trust in Him and He will do this: He will make your righteousness shine like the dawn, the justice of your cause

---

3. The entire chapter is excellent for tough times.

like the noonday sun. Be still before the Lord and wait patiently for Him; do not fret when men succeed in their ways, when they carry out their wicked schemes."

Verses 23–24 say, "If the Lord delights in a man's way, He makes his steps firm; though he stumbles, he will not fall, for the Lord upholds him with His hand" (NIV).

KNOCK, KNOCK!

August 23, 2019

Knock, knock! Who's there? *Opportunity!* Opportunity keeps on knocking. Open the door and take full advantage. Count every game as an opportunity to sharpen your skills as well as show off your skills. Win or lose, you win!

Always remember Joshua 1:9 (TLB) says, "Yes, be bold and strong! Banish fear and doubt! For remember, the Lord your God is with you wherever you go."

Battle cry: "I am bold and strong! I banish fear and doubt! I always remember the Lord my God is with me wherever I go!" (Joshua 1:9, TLB).

Another Audition!

August 29, 2019

There is nothing to fear. This is what you have been waiting to do all of your life! Never compare yourself to anyone else. Just go on that field and be the best Elijah you can be. God is with you because He put this dream in your heart.

If God is for us, who cares who is against us! With God, we win every time in His time and in His way! "Wait for the Lord, be strong and take heart and wait for the Lord" (Psalm 27:14, NIV).

Joshua 1:9 (NIV) says, "Have I not commanded you? Be strong and courageous. Do not be terrified; do not be discouraged, for the Lord your God will be with you wherever you go."

Battle cry: "I am bold and strong! I banish fear and doubt! I remember the Lord, my God is with me wherever I go" (Joshua 1:9, TLB).

Go, Broncos! Win, Broncos! Come on, Jesus!

Extraordinary Things

August 29, 2019

What extraordinary things have you experienced? What have you seen that has filled you with awe and amazement? Is it a prayer that has been answered? Has a passage in the bible met a need in your soul recently? Have you experienced God's forgiveness and grace? Have you seen love demonstrated? Do you marvel at God's power in nature? Has God provided comfort or strength in a time of need?

How do you respond to these extraordinary things? May we always remember to thank God, give Him the glory, and tell what God has done for us.

PROTECTED! (2)

September 9, 2019

Psalm 91:14–15 says, "Because He loves me, says the Lord, I will rescue him; I will protect him, for he acknowledges my name. He will call on me and I will answer him; I will be with him in trouble, I will deliver him and honor him" (NIV).

Keeping my focus on God protects me. I am the director of my thoughts. At times my attention may dwell on old messages I hear in my head. Yet Spirit reminds me that I have the ability to focus my attention on the divine truth available to me through my oneness with God.

I focus on divine love within me, and any illusion I have of being alone or afraid is eradicated! Focused on God, I am at peace!

Let the Games Begin

September 9, 2019

"Even though I walk through the valley of the shadow of death, I will fear no evil for You are with me" (Psalm 23:4, NIV).

You have allowed me to play with the professional and the famous. I am in line, waiting my turn. My job is to be sure I am fit mentally, physically, and spiritually. Waiting takes patience, and it is difficult, but good things come to those who wait. When my name is called, I will be ready, willing, and able to *get in the game*!

"I am still confident of this: I will see the goodness of the Lord in the land of the living. Wait for the Lord; be strong and take heart and wait for the Lord" (Psalm 27:13–14, NIV). Never forget: "Have I not commanded you? Be strong and courageous. Do not be terrified; do not be discouraged, for the Lord your God will be with you wherever you go" (Joshua 1:9, NIV).

Battle cry: "I am bold and strong! I banish fear and doubt! I always remember the Lord my God is with me wherever I go" (Joshua 1:9, TLB).

An Attitude of Gratitude!

September 14, 2019

Psalm 100:4–5 (TLB) says, "Go through His gates with great thanksgiving; enter His courts with praise. Give thanks to Him and bless His name. For the Lord is always good. He is always loving and kind, and His faithfulness goes on and on to each succeeding generation."

"My life is filled with an overflowing measure of God's blessings. I am grateful, and I give thanks to God. His divine healing energy flows through my body, and I embrace the peace that washes over me when challenges appear…The practice of gratitude draws more abundance ever to me. My spirit is at peace and fulfilled."[4]

Always remember Joshua 1:9 (TLB), "Yes, be bold and strong! Banish fear and doubt! For remember, the Lord your God is with you wherever you go."

Go, Broncos! Win, Broncos! Stay in the hunt! Come on, Jesus!

---

4. Excerpt from DW, December 7, 2017

Be Grateful, Be Humble
September 14, 2019

As always, be the best Elijah you can be. Be grateful! Be humble! You are truly living your dream! You are in Colorado playing for the Denver Broncos at Empower Field at Mile High!

First Peter 5:5–8 (GNT) says, "In the same way you younger people must submit yourselves to your elders. And all of you must put on the apron of humility, to serve one another; for the Scripture says, 'God resists the proud, but shows favor to the humble.' Humble yourselves, then, under God's mighty hand, so that he will lift you up in His own good time. Leave all your worries with Him, because He cares for you. Be alert, be on watch! Your enemy, the devil, roams around like a roaring lion, looking for someone to devour. Be firm in your faith and resist him."

Be blessed and give thanks to God!

Joshua 1:9 (NIV) says, "Have I not commanded you? Be strong and courageous! Do not be discouraged; do not be terrified, for the Lord your God is with you wherever you go."

Go, Broncos! Win, Broncos! Stay in the hunt! Come on, Jesus!

PREDESTINED!

September 29, 2019

Predestine: To decree beforehand, to order beforehand

It is not about you! You are living out the destiny God had placed in you before you were born. He has given you His Holy Spirit to keep you wise and spiritually strong. The physical is up to you. He gave you the body, but you must keep it fit. Now that you know who you are, live out your destiny God's way! Bring it on, Jaguars!

Joshua 1:9 (NIV) says, "Have I not commanded you? Be strong and courageous! Do not be discouraged; for the Lord your God is with you wherever you go."

Battle cry: "I am bold and strong! I banish fear and doubt! I remember the Lord my God is with me wherever I go!"

Go, Broncos! Win, Broncos! Stay in the hunt! Come on, Holy Spirit!

Another Chance!

October 6, 2019

Another chance to be at your best.

Galatians 6:9 (AMPC) says, "And let us not lose heart and grow weary and faint in acting nobly and doing right, for in due time and at the appointed season we shall reap, if we do not loosen and relax our courage and faint."

Another chance to show up and be the best *Elijah* you can be!

Joshua 1:9 (NIV) says, "Have I not commanded you? Be strong and courageous! Do not be discouraged; for the Lord your God is with you wherever you go."

Battle cry: "I am bold and strong! I banish fear and doubt! I remember the Lord my God is with me wherever I go!"

Go, Broncos! Win, Broncos! Stay in the hunt! Come on, Holy Spirit!

IMAGINATION!

October 17, 2019

Imagination: Power of forming pictures in the mind of things not present to the senses.

Hope is a positive imagination. Hope activates faith. Faith will make it a reality. Once you get it into your imagination, your vision will bring it into being. "Where there is no vision, the people perish" (Proverbs 29:18, KJV). See with your spiritual eyes!

You have the faith of God inside of you. You have got to see it on the inside before you can see it on the outside.

Take this Word and let it paint a picture on the inside of you! *See it! Do it!*

See yourself handling your man easily, then helping your brothers!

Joshua 1:9 (NIV) says, "Have I not commanded you? Be strong and courageous! Do not be discouraged; for the Lord your God is with you wherever you go."

Battle cry: "I am bold and strong! I banish fear and doubt! I remember the Lord my God is with me wherever I go!"

Go, Broncos! Win, Broncos! Stay in the hunt! Come on, Holy Spirit!

Our Awesome God!

November 2, 2019

We serve an awesome God! God wants to paint a picture of destiny, purpose, and meaning on the pages of your life.

An awesome picture: Look at you playing in the NFL in Denver with you, Odah, and your Aunt Vi coming from Philadelphia to watch you. Don't get distracted! We are here to strengthen you.

Keep walking towards God, and you will walk into your destiny. Your gifts are making room for you.

Be bold! Be brave and strong, for the Lord your God is in every battle with you.

Joshua 1:9 (NIV) says, "Have I not commanded you? Be strong and courageous! Do not be discouraged; for the Lord your God is with you wherever you go."

Battle cry: "I am bold and strong! I banish fear and doubt! I remember the Lord my God is with me wherever I go!"

Come on, Jesus! Come on, Holy Spirit! Win, Broncos!

BREAKTHROUGH!

November 16, 2019

Breakthrough: A military attack that gets through the enemy defensive system into the area in the rear. 2) An achievement or solution of some problem, often of a scientific or technical nature.

What comes after the breakthrough? Another breakthrough! You did it before, you can do it again. In fact, you can do it better than before. See yourself in your mind's eye performing better than you did in your last game. Always compete with yourself.

Get in the *zone*! Get in the *Spirit*! "…Not by might nor by power, but by my *spirit* says the Lord Almighty" (Zechariah 4:6, NIV). "Get in the Spirit through His Word. Keep the Word in your thoughts and in your mouth and the Spirit will obey." He knows the Word of God! "As a man thinks in his heart, so is he" (Proverbs 23:7, KJV). "Let the word of God dwell in you richly" (Colossians 3:16, NIV).

Today, be the best Elijah the world has ever seen!

Never forget!

Joshua 1:9 (NIV) says, "Have I not commanded you? Be strong and courageous; do not be terrified; or discouraged, for the Lord your God will be with you wherever you go."

Battle cry: "I am bold and strong! I banish fear and doubt! I remember the Lord my God is with me wherever I go!"

Come on, Jesus! Come on, Holy Spirit! Win, Broncos!

Focus!

November 23, 2019

Focus: To concentrate. To focus one's attention (Webster).

Stay focused! Do not be distracted by anything. You came to win. Do all that winning requires. Stay in the game, body, soul, and spirit. If distracted, refocus! If negative talk or thoughts occur, replace them with winning talk and thoughts. "I can do all things through Christ Who strengthens me" Philippians 4:13 (KJV). I have strength for all things in Christ, who empowers me. I am ready for anything and equal to anything through Him, who infuses inner strength into me (that is, I am self-sufficient in Christ's sufficiency). Say what God says about you. Your mouth can overpower your mind. Your input determines your output. Stay in the Spirit! Stay in the *zone*! The Holy Spirit can bring out of you what is required to be victorious because He put it in you! Send those Bills where the Buffalos roam!

Joshua 1:9 (NIV) says, "Have I not commanded you? Be strong and courageous; do not be terrified; or discouraged, for the Lord your God will be with you wherever you go."

Battle cry: "I am bold and strong! I banish fear and doubt! I remember the Lord my God is with me wherever I go!"

Come on, Jesus! Come on, Holy Spirit! Win, Broncos!

The Broncos will send those Bills where the Buffalos roam!

Commandment #7: Do not celebrate before the win is in! (Don't even think about it!)

EXPECTATIONS

November 30, 2019

Expectations: Looking for as due, proper or necessary.

What do you expect? You expect a win. A win is due, proper, and necessary! Keep winning in your mouth, in your mind, and in your heart. Don't speak anything you don't want to happen.

Many times when you start believing God, matters get worse. You can't let anything change the belief of truth in your head. The Word of God is truth. Do you have the boldness to speak His truth under pressure? "The word is near you; it is in your mouth and in your heart" (Romans 10:8, NIV). When under pressure, do not change your expectation. Keep the Word in your mouth and in your heart. "For as he thinketh in his heart, so is he..." (Proverbs 23:7, KJV).

Think: "I am bold and strong! I banish fear and doubt. For the Lord my God is with me wherever I go."

Psalm 98:1 says, "O sing unto the Lord a new song, for He has done wonderful things, His right hand and His holy arm have gained the victory for me (Him)" (NASB).

Joshua 1:9 says, "Have I not commanded you? Be strong and courageous. Do not be terrified; do not be discouraged, for the Lord your God is with you wherever you go."

Battle cry: "I am bold and strong! I banish fear and doubt! I remember the Lord my God is with me wherever I go!"

Come on, Jesus! Come on, Holy Spirit! Go, Broncos! Win, Broncos!

Keep Showing up and Showing Out
December 12, 2019

"But the fruit of the Spirit is love, joy, peace, forbearance, kindness, goodness, faithfulness, gentleness and self-control. Against such things there is no law" (Galatians 5:22, NIV).

Do not envy anyone! You are in the right place and in the right position. When you see someone in front of you or beside you doing well, believe that your turn is next! Be grateful for the chances you have to show up and show out. Wait and watch for every chance. Your job is to be ready. You are on standby for the Broncos like the Holy Spirit is on standby for you.

Don't get drunk on wine or smoke; get drunk on the Holy Spirit! Pray always. Pray in the Spirit! If you don't know how, pray and make some sounds with your mouth! Believe when you pray! "Then Jesus told His disciples a parable to show them that they should pray and not give up" (Luke 18:1, NIV).

Destiny!

December 14, 2019

Destiny: The inevitable or necessary succession of events. What will happen, believed to be determined beforehand. The power that is believed to determine the course of events.

God has a plan for you. He is ordering your steps and orchestrating your life. "Before I formed you in the womb I knew you, before you were born I set you apart" (Jeremiah 1:5, NIV).

Jeremiah 29:11 says, "'For I know the plans I have for you,' declares the Lord, plans to prosper you and not to harm you, plans to give you hope and a future."

You are living out the destiny God had put in you before you were born. He has given you His Holy Spirit to keep you wise and Spiritually strong. The physical and mental are up to you. He gave you the body and the mind, but you must keep them fit. Now that you know who you are, live out your destiny God's way! Keep His Word in your mouth and on your mind.

Psalm 91:11–13 (NIV) says, "For He will command His angels concerning you to guard you in all your ways; they will lift you up in their hands, so that you will not strike your foot on a stone. You will tread upon the lion and the cobra, you will trample the great lion and the serpent."

Never forget:

Joshua 1:9 (NIV) "Have I not commanded you? Be strong and courageous! Do not be terrified; or discouraged, for the Lord your God will be with you wherever you go."

Battle cry: "I am bold and strong! I banish fear and doubt! I remember the Lord my God is with me wherever I go."

Come on, Jesus! Come on, Holy Spirit! Go, Broncos! Win, Broncos!

SPEAK IT!

December 21, 2019

It is the Spirit that gives life. He is the life-giver; the flesh conveys no benefit whatever; there is no profit in it. The Words (truths) that I have been speaking to you are Spirit and life. Therefore, speak His Word: "I am bold and strong! I banish fear and doubt! I always remember the Lord my God is with me wherever I go!"

Start living from the inside out. This means praying in the Spirit. You make the noise, the Spirit supplies the words. Getting into the Spirit is a place where you leave your five senses behind. An athlete calls this getting into the "zone."

Take this Word and let it paint a picture in your mind! *Speak it! See it! Do it!* "I have strength for all things in Christ, who empowers me. I am ready for anything and equal to anything through Him, who infuses inner strength into me [that is, I am self-sufficient in Christ's sufficiency]..." (Philippians 4:13, AMPL). See yourself handling your man easily, then helping your brother!

Always remember:

Joshua 1:9 (NIV) says, "Have I not commanded you? Be strong and courageous! Do not be terrified; do not be discouraged, for the Lord your God will be with you wherever you go."

Battle cry: "I am bold and strong! I banish fear and doubt! I remember the Lord my God is with me wherever I go!"

Come on, Jesus! Come on, Holy Spirit! Go, Broncos! Win, Broncos!

Untitled

November 9, 2019

Dear Grandson,

The last two pictures, one from the Denver Post and one from the Broncos' website, have prompted me to write you. They suggest to me that you are downcast in Spirit. Always remember who is living inside of your spirit. He lives inside of you, and He brings the fruit of the Spirit: love, joy, peace, patience, kindness, goodness, faithfulness, gentleness, and self-control into your life. Use your faith to be patient. You are on a journey with Him. No one can take your good from you. What God has planned for you will come if you wait on Him. With every wait, there is a suddenly! Rec all some of your *suddenlies*! As an old lady once told me, "I dare you to trust Him!" Now your old grandmom is telling you, "I dare you to trust Him!"

Love and blessings always,

Odah and your grandmom

Scriptures: Psalm 37:4–7, 23–24. (The entire chapter is excellent for tough times.)

"Delight yourself in the Lord and He will give you the desires of your heart. Commit your way to the Lord; trust in Him and He will do this: He will make your righteousness shine like the dawn, the justice of your cause like the noonday sun. Be still before the

Lord and wait patiently for Him; do not fret when men succeed in their ways, when they carry out their wicked schemes." Verses 23–24 say, "If the Lord delights in a man's way, He makes his steps firm; though he stumble, he will not fall, for the Lord upholds him with His hand."

Knock! Knock! (2)

August 23, 2019

Who's there? *Opportunity!* Opportunity keeps on knocking. Open the door and take full advantage. Count every game as an opportunity to sharpen your skills as well as show off your skills. Win or lose, you win!

Always remember:

Joshua 1:9 (TLB) says, "Yes, be bold and strong! Banish fear and doubt! For remember, the Lord your God is with you wherever you go."

Battle cry: "I am bold and strong! I banish fear and doubt! I always remember the Lord my God is with me wherever I go!"

Another Audition! (2)

August 29, 2019

There is nothing to fear. This is what you have been waiting to do all of your life! Never compare yourself to anyone else. Just go on that field and be the best Elijah you can be. God is with you because He put this dream in your heart. "If God is for us, who can be against us?" (Romans 8:31, NIV). If God is for us, who cares who is against us! With God, we win every time in His time and in His way! "Wait for the Lord, be strong and take heart and wait for the Lord" (Psalm 27:14, NIV).

Joshua 1:9 (NIV) says, "Have I not commanded you? Be strong and courageous. Do not be terrified; do not be discouraged, for the Lord your God will be with you wherever you go."

Battle cry: "I am bold and strong! I banish fear and doubt! I remember the Lord my God is with me wherever I go."

Come on, Jesus! Come on, Holy Spirit! Go, Broncos! Win, Broncos!

EXTRAORDINARY THINGS

August 29, 2019

What extraordinary things have you experienced? What have you seen that has filled you with awe and amazement? Is it a prayer that has been answered? Has a passage in the bible met a need in your soul recently? Have you experienced God's forgiveness and grace? Have you seen love demonstrated? Do you marvel at God's power in nature? Has God provided comfort or strength in a time of need?

How do you respond to these extraordinary things? May we always remember to thank God, give Him the glory, and tell what God has done for us.

PROTECTED!

September 9, 2019

Psalm 91:14–15 says, "Because He loves me, says the Lord, I will rescue him; I will protect him, for he acknowledges my name. He will call upon me and I will answer him; I will be with him in trouble, I will deliver him and honor him."

Keeping my focus on God protects me. I am the director of my thoughts. At times my attention may dwell on old messages I hear in my head. Yet Spirit reminds me that I have the ability to focus my attention on the divine truth available to me through my oneness with God.

I focus on divine love within me, and any illusion I have of being alone or afraid is eradicated! Focused on God, I am at peace!

Let the Games Begin! (2)
September 9, 2019

"Even though I walk through the valley of the shadow of death, I will fear no evil for You are with me" (Psalm 23:4, NIV).

You have allowed me to play with the professional and the famous. I am in line, waiting my turn. My job is to be sure I am fit mentally, physically, and spiritually. Waiting takes patience, and it is difficult, but good things come to those who wait. When my name is called, I will be ready, willing, and able to *get in the game*!

"I am still confident of this: I will see the goodness of the Lord in the land of the living. Wait for the Lord; be strong and take heart and wait for the Lord" (Psalm 27:13–14, NIV).

Never forget: "Have I not commanded you? Be strong and courageous. Do not be terrified; do not be discouraged, for the Lord your God will be with you wherever you go" (Joshua 1:9, NIV).

Battle cry: I am bold and strong! I banish fear and doubt! I always remember the Lord my God is with me wherever I go!"

The Dream Continues!

September 13, 2020

"I will exalt you, Lord, for you lifted me out of the depths and did not let my enemies gloat over me. Lord my God, I called to you for help, and you healed me" (Psalm 30:1–2, NIV).

Thank you, Lord, for bringing me to this day to continue my dream of the fourth year with the Denver Broncos in good health and strength. In addition, you have blessed me with a family of my own. With your help, I have become stronger, wiser, and better in many ways. I am stronger in the Lord. "I can do all things through Christ who strengthens me" (Philippians 4:13, NKJV). Lord, you have brought me this far, and I trust you to take me all the way safely with honor. My dream is to complete this journey with you!

Don't forget:

Joshua 1:9 (NIV) says, "Have I not commanded you? Be strong and courageous! Do not be discouraged; do not be terrified, for the Lord your God is with you wherever you go."

Battle cry: "I am bold and strong! I banish fear and doubt! I remember the Lord my God is with me wherever I go!" (Joshua 1:9, TLB).

Come on, Jesus! Come on, Holy Spirit! Go, Broncos! Win, Broncos!

Be Grateful, Be Humble (2)

September 14, 2019

As always, be the best Elijah you can be. Be grateful! Be humble! You are truly living your dream! You are in Colorado playing for the Denver Broncos at Empower Field at Mile High! First Peter 5:5–8 (GNT) says, "In the same way you younger people must submit yourselves to your elders. And all of you must put on the apron of humility, to serve one another; for the Scripture says, 'God resists the proud, but shows favor to the humble.' Humble yourselves, then, under God's mighty hand, so that he will lift you up in His own good time. Leave all your worries with Him, because He cares for you."

Be alert, be on watch! Your enemy, the devil, roams around like a roaring lion, looking for someone to devour. Be firm in your faith and resist him,"

Be blessed and give thanks to God!

Joshua 1:9 (NIV) says, "Have I not commanded you? Be strong and courageous! Do not be discouraged; do not be terrified, for the Lord your God is with you wherever you go."

Go, Broncos! Win, Broncos! Stay in the hunt! Come on, Jesus!

PREDESTINED!

September 29, 2019

Predestine: To decree beforehand, to order beforehand,

It is not about you! You are living out the destiny God had placed in you before you were born. He has given you His Holy Spirit to keep you wise and spiritually strong. The physical is up to you. He gave you the body, but you must keep it fit. Now that you know who you are, live out your destiny God's way! Bring it on, Jaguars!

Joshua 1:9 (NIV) says, "Have I not commanded you? Be strong and courageous! Do not be discouraged; for the Lord your God is with you wherever you go."

Battle cry: "I am bold and strong! I banish fear and doubt! I remember the Lord my God is with me wherever I go!"

Go, Broncos! Win, Broncos! Stay in the hunt! Come on, Holy Spirit!

Another Chance!

October 6, 2019

Another chance to be at your best.

Galatians 6:9 (AMP) says, "And let us not lose heart and grow weary and faint in acting nobly and doing right, for in due time and at the appointed season we shall reap, if we do not loosen and relax our courage and faint."

Another chance to show up and be the best *Elijah* you can be!

"Have I not commanded you? Be strong and courageous! Do not be discouraged; do not be terrified, for the Lord your God is with you wherever you go" (Joshua 1:9, NIV).

Battle cry: "I am bold and strong! I banish fear and doubt! I remember the Lord, my God, is with me wherever I go" (Joshua 1:9, TLB),

Go, Broncos! Win, Broncos! Come on, Jesus! Come on, Holy Spirit!

Destiny! (2)

December 14, 2019

Destiny: The inevitable or necessary succession of events. What will happen, believed to be determined beforehand. The power that is believed to determine the course of events.

God has a plan for you. He is ordering your steps and orchestrating your life.

Jeremiah 1:5 (NIV) says, "Before I formed you in the womb I knew you, before you were born I set you apart..." Jeremiah 29:11 says, "'For I know the plans I have for you,' declares the Lord, plans to prosper you and not to harm you, plans to give you hope and a future."

You are living out the destiny God put in you before you were born. He has given you His Holy Spirit to keep you wise and Spiritually strong. The physical and mental are up to you. He gave you the body and the mind, but you must keep them fit. Now that you know who you are, live out your destiny God's way! Keep His Word in your mouth and on your mind.

Psalm 91:11–13 (NIV) says, "For He will command His angels concerning you to guard you in all your ways; they will lift you up in their hands, so that you will not strike your foot on a stone. You will tread upon the lion and the cobra, you will trample the great lion and the serpent."

Never forget:

Joshua 1:9 (NIV) says, "Have I not commanded you? Be strong and courageous! Do not be terrified; or discouraged, for the Lord your God will be with you wherever you go."

Battle cry: "I am bold and strong! I banish fear and doubt! I remember the Lord my God is with me wherever I go."

Come on, Jesus! Come on, Holy Spirit! Come on, Broncos! Win, Broncos!

Rejoice and Believe!

December 19, 2020

When I think about what God has done, is doing, and will do in my life, I can think of myself happy and joyful! When my brother is being blessed, I am not jealous. I rejoice with him because I know that my turn is next if I only believe. It is my job to keep working hard, doing my best, and believing. It is God's job to make it happen! "Wait patiently for the Lord. Be brave and courageous. Yes, wait patiently for the Lord" (Psalm 27:14, NLT).

Now is the time to do your job! Go on that Empower Field at Mile High and work hard, do your best, and keep on believing!

Never forget!

Joshua 1:9 (NIV) says, "Have I not commanded you? Be strong and courageous. Do not be terrified; do not be discouraged, for the Lord your God is with you wherever you go."

Battle cry: "I am bold and strong! I banish fear and doubt! I remember the Lord, my God, is with me wherever I go" (Joshua 1:9, TLB).

Come on, Jesus! Come on, Holy Spirit! Go, Broncos! Win, Broncos!

Speak It!

December 21, 2019

"It is the Spirit Who gives life [He is the Life-giver]; the flesh conveys no benefit whatever [there is no profit in it]. The words (truths) that I have been speaking to you are spirit and life" (John 6:63, AMPC). Therefore, speak His Word: "I am bold and strong! I banish fear and doubt! I always remember the Lord, my God, is with me wherever I go!"

Start living from the inside out. This means praying in the Spirit. You make the noise, the Spirit supplies the words. Getting into the Spirit is a place where you leave your five senses behind. An athlete calls this getting "into the zone."

Take this Word and let it paint a picture in your mind! *Speak it! See it! Do it!* "I have strength for all things in Christ, who empowers me. I am ready for anything and equal to anything through Him, who infuses inner strength into me [that is, I am self-sufficient in Christ's sufficiency]…" (Philippians 4:13, AMP). See yourself handling your man easily, then helping your brother!

Always remember:

Joshua 1:9 (NIV) says, "Have I not commanded you? Be strong and courageous! Do not be terrified; do not be discouraged, for the Lord your God will be with you wherever you go.

Battle cry: "I am bold and strong! I banish fear and doubt! I remember the Lord, my God, is with me wherever I go" (Joshua 1:9, TLB).

Come on, Jesus! Come on, Holy Spirit! Go, Broncos! Win, Broncos!

Patience!

September 26, 2020

Patience: The will or ability to wait or endure without complaint; steadiness, endurance, or perseverance in performing a task.

"And let us not lose heart and grow weary and faint in acting nobly and doing right, for in due time and at the appointed season we shall reap, if we do not loosen and relax our courage and faint" (Galatians 6:9, AMPC).

Continue to thank God and praise him that you are able to perform this season just like you had planned. Continue to do what no one else can do: Be the best *Elijah* you can be! Handle your man, then help your brothers!

"I will praise you, Lord, for you have saved me from my enemies. You refuse to let them triumph over me. O Lord my God, I pleaded with you, and you gave me my health again" (Psalm 30:1–2, TLB).

Thank you, Lord, for your many blessings. "Surely your goodness and unfailing love will pursue me all the days of my life, and I will live in the house of the Lord forever" (Psalm 23:6, NLT).

Never forget!

Joshua 1:9 (NIV) says, "Have I not commanded you? Be strong and courageous. Do not be terrified; do not be discouraged, for the Lord your God will be with you wherever you go."

Battle cry: "I am bold and strong! I banish fear and doubt! I remember the Lord my God is with me wherever I go!" (Joshua 1:9, TLB).

Come on, Jesus! Come on, Holy Spirit! Go, Broncos! Win, Broncos!

October 4, 2020

Dear Grandson,

I have been thinking about you and the injuries to your left leg. I only know about football injuries from your Granddad and you. I wasn't around when he was injured, but I got to live with them when he came home from Germany, where he played football for the United States Air Force. He never regretted them. As a matter of fact, he tried to play for Temple University when he came home, but he couldn't afford it. They couldn't afford to give him a football scholarship, and he needed money to continue his education. He was forced to work to continue his education. He worked his way through Temple and earned three degrees.

When he came home from Germany, he brought with him scars from football and the Vietnam War. His left arm is wired on at the shoulder. I know you have seen that scar. He had bad knees also. He had at least three knee surgeries since we were married. He also had about three back surgeries since we were married. Those are his football injuries. His war injuries are not visible. As you can see, we have been through a lot together.

I am telling you all this so that you will know that injuries come with the job. I don't know what you are thinking about your injuries, but you can see he wasn't going to let his injuries stop him from doing what he loved. He even started grooming you when he saw your aptitude for football and your love for it. He loved being involved with your growth as you pursued your dream to play for the NFL, and you know how much he loved you! You were his heart walking outside his body.

If you love football like your Granddad, take your scars and keep fighting! If you are having regrets, you can take what you have earned and retire from football.

As your grandmom, I am here to support and guide you on whatever path you choose. I will listen and let you decide what you will do. It's your life, and you have to live it. I thank God that He allowed us to live to see you succeed in your dream. Now, I will live to see my great-granddaughter through you and Gabrielle. Don't worry, you will have sons!

Blessings and love forever,

Your Odah and your grandmom

Why We Have the Authority to Say, "Be Healed in the Name of Jesus"

October 10, 2020

Mark 16:15–18 (NLT) says, "Jesus speaking to the eleven disciples after He had been raised from the dead: "And then he told them, 'Go into all the world and preach the Good News to everyone. Anyone who believes and is baptized will be saved. But anyone who refuses to believe will be condemned.' These miraculous signs will accompany those who believe: They will cast out demons in my name, and they will speak in new languages. They will be able to handle snakes with safety, and if they drink anything poisonous, it won't hurt them. They will be able to place their hands on the sick, and they will be healed."

John 14:12–14 (NIV) says, "I tell you the truth, anyone who has faith in me will do what I have been doing. He will do even greater things than these, because I am going to the Father.

And I will do whatever you ask in my name, so that the Son may bring glory to the Father. You may ask me for anything in my name, and I will do it."

Jesus promises the Holy Spirit, "If you love me, obey my commandments. And I will ask the Father, and he will give you another Advocate, who will never leave you. He is the Holy Spirit, who leads into all truth. The world cannot receive him, because it isn't looking for him and doesn't recognize him. But you know him, because he lives with you now and later will be in you" (John 14:15–17, NLT).

Jesus sends out the Twelve: "They went out and preached that people should repent. They drove out many demons and anointed many sick people with oil and healed them" (Mark 6:12–13, NIV).

Jesus heals many: "When the sun was setting, the people brought to Jesus all who had various kinds of sickness, and laying his hands on each one, he healed them" (Luke 4:40, NIV).

Faith in the Son of God, "This is the confidence we have in approaching God: that if we ask anything according to his will, he hears us. And if we know that He hears us—whatever we ask—we know that we have what we asked of Him" (1 John 5:14–15, NIV).

The Waiting Room

October 18, 2020

You are in the waiting room! You are not missing out. God has you right where He wants you. Waiting doesn't mean nothing is happening, or God has forgotten you. You have to pass the test in the waiting room. Do your best while you wait. If it is not working out, God is working something out of you. Courage, strength, and endurance are developing in the waiting room. Something is happening: you are growing and developing. Keep a good attitude when it is not happening as fast as you would like. Sometimes God proves His love to us by not giving us what we want. God, don't give me anything that I don't have the grace to handle. What has your name on it is coming your way. What God has for you is on the way. It's taking longer because it is greater than you expect. Stay in faith, and you will see God has something better. You are waiting for something big and out of the ordinary. God is about to open a door that you didn't see coming. Keep being your best! What has your name on it can't go to someone else. When it is taking longer than you thought, something big and unexpected is coming. When you don't get impatient or jealous, God will give you the position! He is going to put your name on something bigger and better. Sometimes, God will not let you see something now because He is preparing something that you didn't see coming!

LIVING A GRATEFUL LIFE

November 22, 2020

First Thessalonians 5:18 (NASB) says, "In everything give thanks; for this is God's will for you in Christ Jesus." The same verse (AMPC) says, "No matter what the circumstances may be, be thankful and give thanks..." Be thankful for where you are right now. It is the will of God for you. Learn to be content where you are right now. Be appreciative of what God has done for you. Rich in love, joy, fellowship; these are the things for which you should be thankful. Learn to be thankful for the small things, and you will be promoted. You will be so blessed that you will know nobody but God has done it!

"Have I not commanded you? Be strong and courageous. Do not be terrified; do not be discouraged, for the Lord your God will be with you wherever you go" (Joshua 1:9, NIV).

Battle cry: "I am bold and strong! I banish fear and doubt! I remember the Lord my God is with me wherever I go!" (Joshua 1:9, TLB).

Come on, Jesus! Come on, Holy Spirit! Go, Broncos! Win, Broncos!

WAITING ROOM (2)

November 28, 2020

Wait: To stay in place or remain inactive until something expected takes place.

Psalm 27:14 (NASB) says, "Wait for the Lord; Be strong, and let your heart take courage. Yes, wait for the Lord."

Waiting is a time for growth, renewal, healing, repair, and rest. Try not to grow impatient in the waiting room, for it is also a place for protection. While you are there, your exposure to COVID-19 is limited! Remember J. J., the right tackle you replaced, took leave to protect his baby. You have a baby daughter to protect now. Who knows that such a time as this waiting was planned for the protection of you and your family.

You are not missing out. God has you right where He wants you. Waiting doesn't mean nothing is happening, or God has forgotten you. You have to pass the test in the waiting room. Do your best while you wait. Courage, strength, and endurance are developing in the waiting room. Something is happening: you are growing and developing. Keep a good attitude when it is not happening as fast as you would like. What has your name on it is coming your way. What God has for you is on the way. It's taking longer because it is greater than you expect. God is about to open a door that you didn't see coming. Keep being your best! What has your name on it can't go to someone else. When it is taking longer than you thought, something big and unexpected is coming. When you don't get impatient or jealous, God will give you the position! He is going to put your name on something that you didn't see coming!

"Yet those who wait for the Lord will gain new strength; They will mount up with wings like eagles, They will run and not get tired, They will walk and not become weary" (Isaiah 40:31, NASB).

"The Lord is good to those who wait for Him, To the person who seeks Him" (Lamentations 3:25, NASB).

Answered Prayer!

December 6, 2020

Your prayer was to finish strong and make some good tapes. You are given the opportunity to make some good tapes by playing against some good teams. Today, you have the opportunity to play against the formidable Kansas City Chiefs! Go handle those Chiefs and make your good tapes!

First John 5:14 (NIV) says, "This is the confidence we have in approaching God: that if we ask anything according to his will, he hears us. And if we know that He hears us—whatever we ask—we know that we have what we asked of Him."

Be blessed and give thanks to God!

Don't forget:

Joshua 1:9 (NIV) says, "Have I not commanded you? Be strong and courageous. Do not be terrified; do not be discouraged, for the Lord your God will be with you wherever you go."

Battle cry: "I am bold and strong! I banish fear and doubt! I remember the Lord my God is with me wherever I go!" (Joshua 1:9, TLB).

Come on, Jesus! Come on, Holy Spirit! Go, Broncos! Win, Broncos!

A Prayer for Elijah

December 26, 2020

Now that you are able to be back on the active roster, change your prayer. As you lay hands on your left ankle and left shin, pray:

Thank you, Jesus, for healing my ankle.

Thank you, Jesus, for healing my shin.

Thank you, Jesus, for healing me!

If a fresh injury occurs, lay hands on it immediately and pray, "Be healed in the name of Jesus!"

"Be joyful always; pray continually; give thanks in all circumstances for this is God's will for you in Christ Jesus" (1 Thessalonians 5:16–18, NIV).

Order My Steps

January 3, 2021

Psalm 37:23–24 (NIV) says, "The Lord directs the steps of the godly. He delights in every detail of their lives. Though they stumble, they will never fall, for the Lord holds them by the hand." God orders your steps. He has it all figured out. He doesn't always take you on a straight path. Do your best and trust Him! Just keep moving forward, taking one step at a time. Empty out the negative from yesterday and the last game and start this day in faith. Enjoy this day, enjoy this game! "This is the day the Lord has made; let us rejoice and be glad in it. O Lord, save us; O Lord, grant us success. Blessed is he who comes in the name of the Lord" (Psalm 118:24–26, NIV).

"I pursued my enemies and overtook them; I did not turn back until they were destroyed. I crushed them so that they could not rise; they fell beneath my feet. You armed me with strength for battle; you made my adversaries bow at my feet. You made my enemies turn their backs in flight, and I destroyed my foes" (Psalm 18:37–40, NIV).

Always remember:

Joshua 1:9 (NIV) says, "Have I not commanded you? Be strong and courageous! Do not be terrified; do not be discouraged, for the Lord your God will be with you wherever you go."

Battle cry: "I am bold and strong! I banish fear and doubt! I remember the Lord my God is with me wherever I go!" (Joshua 1:9, TLB).

Come on, Jesus! Come on, Holy Spirit! Go, Broncos! Win, Broncos!

CPSIA information can be obtained
at www.ICGtesting.com
Printed in the USA
BVHW090105100222
628030BV00007B/16

9 781685 561314